CW00664914

2   The hills of the Black Mount reflect in Loch na h-Achlaise on the southern edge of Lochaber.

LOCHABER

A pictorial souvenir

NESS PUBLISHING

LOCHABER

Welcome to Lochaber!

The district of Lochaber dates back to ancient times, the name first appearing in St Adomnan's *Life of Saint Columba*, written in the 690s. It comprises a region of north-western Scotland based on the town of Fort William which is inevitably mountainous and deeply penetrated by numerous sea lochs. The greatest of these is Loch Linnhe, at the head of which stands Fort William. These geographical features make Lochaber a harsh land, one that has never been greatly populated, although some parts were more peopled in former times than now. This shows in Lochaber's population figures, which record more inhabitants in 1801 than 1981. The difficulty of the terrain meant that it was little known by outsiders until the 19th century, when road improvements and (later) railways opened up the region to visitors.

Lochaber is a land of extremes: Ben Nevis, Britain's highest mountain at 1344m/4406ft; Loch Morar, Scotland's deepest loch with a maximum depth of 310m/1015ft; Ardnamurchan Point, the most westerly extremity of the British mainland; to the north, Knoydart, the least populated and most inaccessible part of mainland Britain. It also incorporates the southern third of the Great Glen, possibly the most dramatic feature of Scotland's landscape.

Historically too, Lochaber has seen its share of notable events. Glen Coe witnessed one of Scotland's greatest acts of treachery in the infamous massacre of 1692; in Glenfinnan began the final flowering of Prince Charles Edward Stuart's (Bonnie Prince Charlie's) dream to re-instate

Rough country: from the northern shoulder of Aonach Mor, a view across the gully to **5** Carn Mor Dearg, with the summit of Ben Nevis rising beyond.

the Stuart monarchy. In very different vein, Fort William became a pioneer of renewable energy: in 1896 it was the first town in Britain to be lit by hydro-electric power. The potential for hydro-electricity was one of the main reasons why aluminium smelters were established in Lochaber – this, combined with the sheltered berthing in the sea lochs for ships delivering the raw material. The industry continues to this day in Fort William.

Lochaber is something of an anomaly in these days of local government re-organisations and streamlining. That it remains an administrative district shows how it is defined more by geography than politics. It has never been a respecter of human boundaries, unless you go back to times when people were content to be identified according to the limits of their landscape. In terms of the pre-1974 counties, its northern two-thirds belonged to Inverness-shire while the southern third was in Argyll. Nowadays, it is all part of the Highland Region, which itself has taken over the northernmost parts of Argyll, so that the present-day southern boundary approximates to the historic southerly outline of Lochaber. Despite bureaucratic tinkering, Lochaber remains Lochaber.

This book sets out to illustrate Lochaber by means of a number of journeys from Fort William. As will by now be apparent, this is not an area one can easily circumnavigate, so we shall explore by taking the available routes to the north (including an excursion to the eastern boundary), the west along the Road to the Isles, the southwest via the Corran Ferry to Morvern and Ardnamurchan and the south to Glen Coe and beyond. In this way, it is hoped that readers will gain an appreciation of the differing moods and 'feel' of each constituent part, together with an understanding of how they fit together – the way in which Lochaber as a whole still lives and breathes as a distinct and unique part of Scotland.

Looking out to sea at Loch Nan Uamh. This is where Bonnie Prince Charlie returned to the Scottish mainland in 1745 to lead what proved to be the last Jacobite uprising.

8   Fort William and Ben Nevis viewed across Loch Linnhe from the village of Trislaig. The town's name goes back to 1690 when the rebuilt fort was named in honour of King William of Orange.

At the same time, the adjacent settlement was renamed Maryburgh after his wife, Queen Mary, but it's the name of Fort William that has prevailed.

10 Left: a 'Secret Portrait' of Bonnie Prince Charlie is revealed in the reflecting cylinder, an exhibit at the West Highland Museum in Fort William. Right: the Baptistry in the Episcopal Church, Fort William.

Inverlochy Castle, just north of Fort William, was built by the Comyns of Lochaber **11** in the late 13th century, but lost to Robert the Bruce in 1307.

12 Left: Steall Falls are worth the walk up Glen Nevis. Right: Not surprisingly, Ben Nevis dominates the area and is visible in this view from Treasures of the Earth in Corpach.

Sunset on Loch Linnhe. This great sea loch runs south-west from Fort William **13** for a distance of over 30 miles.

14 Left: an aerial view of the eight locks known as 'Neptune's Staircase' on the Caledonian Canal at Banavie, west of Fort William. Right: a scene on the canal at the top of these locks . . .

. . . and looking in the opposite direction. The Caledonian Canal opened in 1822 **15**
linking Fort William with Inverness at the other end of the Great Glen.

16 Glen Roy. The pointers pick out the 'Parallel Roads', the shorelines of a former loch at three periods in its existence, when the glen was blocked by a glacier.

Looking south from Roy Bridge in Glen Spean at Aonach Beag and Aonach Mor, both over **17** 1220m/4000ft. Aonach Mor is one of Scotland's principal skiing destinations.

18 Continuing up Glen Spean brings us to Lochaber's eastern boundary, another mountainous area as this picture of Coire Ardair, below Creag Meagaidh (1128m/3701ft), shows.

To the right of the scene opposite, the summit of Stob Poite Coire Ardair demonstrates how **19** wind-blown snow forms a 'cornice' over the mountain's edge, a potential danger for climbers.

20 Looking into Lochaber from the east across Loch Laggan, Stob Coire Claurigh rises impressively to 1177m/3862ft. It is the easternmost peak in the Ben Nevis/Grey Corries range.

Left: returning down Glen Spean gives an opportunity to see the Monessie Gorge. Right: memorial **21** near Spean Bridge to the Commandos who trained in this area during the Second World War.

22 Although it makes an idyllic winter scene, this view into Glen Loy gives an idea of what a tough training ground the area would have been for the Commandos.

Back in the Great Glen and travelling north-west, Loch Lochy reflects **23** the craggy outline of Meall nan Dearcag.

24 The empty land of Knoydart is the most northerly part of Lochaber. You cannot get there by road – the nearest one, which skirts Loch Quoich (see p.27), ends at Kinloch Hourn, from where you walk.

By boat from Mallaig (see p.36) to the village of Inverie is another way in. The picture shows Ladhair Bheinn, Knoydart's highest mountain at 1020m/3346ft. **25**

Further up the Great Glen, we look down at another of Lochaber's boundary points, at the northern end of Loch Oich. The Bridge of Oich suspension bridge can be seen in the foreground.

26 The picture looks towards Fort William with Loch Lochy visible in the distance. The Caledonian Canal links Lochs Lochy, Oich and Ness on its way to Inverness.

Such roads as there are in northern Lochaber are accessed by leaving the Great Glen at Invergarry on Loch Oich. Loch Quoich, and Gairich rising beyond it, represent this area.

Part three: the Road to the Isles

28 Our next journey takes the Road to the Isles, which leaves Fort William by following the route along Loch Eil, seen in the distance, and heading west towards Mallaig.

On this route we come to Glenfinnan, where Bonnie Prince Charlie raised his standard and **29** gathered support in 1745. The monument at the head of Loch Shiel commemorates this event.

30   During the summer months, the Jacobite steam-hauled train runs between
       Fort William and Mallaig, seen here crossing Glenfinnan viaduct.

Continuing westwards through the hills reveals Loch Eilt. The Fort William **31** to Mallaig railway can be seen skirting the northern side of the loch.

32 A few miles on is Loch Ailort, above, and the village of the same name, where the road from Moidart (of which more later) joins from the south.

The village of Arisaig enjoys one of the loveliest settings in Lochaber and **33** is seen here from the far side of the bay at the head of which it stands.

34 At Arisaig the route turns north and goes on to Morar, famous for its beautiful white sands.

Just inland from the village of Morar is Loch Morar which stretches inland eastwards **35** for approximately 12 miles. It is the deepest loch in Scotland.

36 The fishing port of Mallaig was created in 1901 after the arrival of the railway. Herring was the main catch but today other fish are more important. Ferries sail to the Hebrides from Mallaig.

Left: the story of the fishwives is one of those told at Mallaig Heritage Centre, as depicted above.
Right: Lochaber's only Lifeboat is based at Mallaig.

38 From the heights of Aonach Mor near Fort William, this view takes in the lands of Ardgour, Morvern and Ardnamurchan away to the south-west, the next areas to be explored.

The best way to Ardgour and beyond is via the Corran Ferry, a few miles south of
Fort William where Loch Linnhe narrows to provide a convenient crossing point.

40 From Glencoe village near Ballachulish and with Loch Leven in the foreground, there is a fine view of the Ardgour mountains, with Garbh Bheinn (meaning 'rough hill') left of centre.

The pass through to Morvern and Ardnamurchan goes round to its left. The picture on p.66 is from the Ardgour side looking back in this direction.

42 The southerly loop off the road to Ardnamurchan takes travellers around the sparsely populated district of Morvern. At the head of Loch Aline stands Ardtornish House, built from 1885 to 1891.

Lochaline is the main village in Morvern, on its southern shore with the island of Mull just **43** a couple of miles away. The ferry (left of picture) to Fishnish on Mull sails from Lochaline.

44 This impressive Celtic cross from the 14th or 15th century stands in Kiel churchyard, just outside Lochaline. This has been a Christian site since the early days of the faith in Scotland.

The interior of St Columba's, Kiel, the church also seen opposite. Built in 1898, it replaced an **45** earlier structure. According to tradition, St Columba established the church in Morvern.

46 The road from Morvern to Ardnamurchan makes its way round the head of Loch Sunart, pictured, to join the 'main' road near the village of Strontian. The Ardgour hills are in the distance.

The road through Ardnamurchan continues west through Salen, which is blessed with this **47** view over Salen Bay, an inlet off Loch Sunart. Across the water is northern Morvern.

48 From near the hamlet of Ardslingnish, a westward view along the shoreline under the slopes of Ben Hiant (see also p.60).

Kilchoan is the next village, location of Ardnamurchan Parish Church. Built 1827-1831 **49** in the Tudor style, it was paid for by the laird, Sir James Riddell.

50 Just outside Kilchoan, Mingary Castle is strategically positioned to guard the end of the Sound of Mull and the entrance to Loch Sunart. Seen here from Kilchoan pier.

Looking across the water from Kilchoan, more inviting scenery beckons travellers onward. **51**

52 And finally the long and winding road brings us to Ardnamurchan Point, 45 miles from the Corran Ferry. The western extremity of the British mainland, it is about as far west as Belfast!

Ardnamurchan Lighthouse was designed by Alan Stevenson, completed in 1849 and is **53** 35m/114ft high. It became automatic in 1988 and today its buildings house a museum.

54 Highland cattle pass a pleasant day grazing on an Ardnamurchan farm.

It really does look like this! No tinkering with the photograph required **55** in this seascape at Sanna Bay, north-east of Ardnamurchan Point.

56 And with extensive soft white sands, on a summer day the beach at Sanna rivals any you care to think of.

As can be seen, a few holidaymakers are enjoying the day, but this must be one of the least exploited seaside spots in Scotland.

58 From Fascadale on the northern side of Ardnamurchan several of the smaller Hebridean islands can be seen. This is the mountainous island of Rum – the sailing boat gives an idea of scale.

Left: the White-Tailed or Sea Eagle was re-introduced to Scotland in 1975. It has an eight-foot wing- **59**
span. Right: the future of the Scottish Wild Cat does not look good – numbers are down to about 400.

60 At 527m/1723ft Ben Hiant is not a huge mountain by Scottish standards but an impressive one nonetheless. It is a remnant of the vast volcano that once dominated the area.

Beautiful Loch Mudle's existence was also shaped by volcanic activity. It is surrounded by **61** flat-lying basalt lavas that flooded from fissures in the rocks.

62 Travelling back eastwards through Ardnamurchan gives the best view of Ben Resipol, the highest point this side of Ardgour at 846m/2766ft.

Striking north now to Acharacle, from where this view takes in the southern end of the 18-mile **63** length of Loch Shiel, last seen on p.29. Beyond this village, we enter the district of Moidart.

64 A testament to the past power of the Lords of the Isles, the remains of Castle Tioram on Loch Moidart still make an impressive sight in a stunning location.

The view north from the castle's rocky islet is of Eilean Shona, **65**
an island held in the surrounding arms of Loch Moidart.

66 Our last journey is south from Fort William to Glen Coe. Here, we look across Loch Linnhe from Ardgour into the jaws of the glen. Note the mountain on the right – Bidean nam Bian.

This beautiful garden is at Onich, where Loch Leven meets Loch Linnhe. **67**
In the background the dark hills of Glen Coe stand guard.

68 A dawn view of Glen Coe from Ballachulish Bridge, with the famous Pap of Glencoe prominent to the left of centre above Loch Leven.

Now up in the heart of Glen Coe, we begin a day in the mountains which will allow a **69** closer look at that little peak towards the left of the picture.

70 The ascent to that point takes walkers through classic mountain territory of streams tumbling over endless rocks. And no, the horizon seen here is not the summit.

Turn your back on the waterfalls and the awesome sight of Aonach Eagach, **71** the 'notched ridge', greets you. This ridge lines the northern side of Glen Coe.

72 Dawn on a winter's day lights up Buachaille Etive Mor, gatekeeper of the south-eastern approach to Glen Coe and one of the most iconic mountains in all of Scotland.

While it is not particularly high at 1021m/3350ft, it is a challenge for hill-walkers and
rock-climbers alike. Its perfect shape from this side adds to its appeal. See also p.77.

74 Meanwhile, back on our ascent of the highest mountain in Glen Coe, these pinnacled buttresses are the preserve of serious rock-climbers. Avoid them by the easier slopes either side. . .

. . . and reach the summit of Stob Coire nan Lochan. Looking north, the first ridge is **75** Aonach Eagach, after which is the Mamore range, and finally Ben Nevis in the distance.

76 To the left, or west, of the previous view, there is a wonderful vista down to Glencoe village, Loch Leven and Loch Linnhe, with Ardgour beyond.

After a short descent and final climb, the 1150m/3773ft summit of Bidean nam Bian is finally attained. **77**
Looking north-east now, to the right in the middle distance is Buachaille Etive Mor's summit.

78 Descending by a different route, into the 'Lost Valley' seen here,
is another way back down into Glen Coe.

Last stop is on the southern edge of Lochaber, where Loch na h-Achlaise reflects the hills of the Black
Mount. Compare this with the picture on pp.2-3. Beyond here – that's the subject of another tour…

Published 2009 by Ness Publishing, 47 Academy Street, Elgin, Moray, IV30 1LR
Phone/fax 01343 549663 www.nesspublishing.co.uk

Second reprint 2011

Reprinted 2010

All photographs © Colin and Eithne Nutt except p.10 (left) © West Highland Museum; pp.14 (left) & 26 © Scotavia Images; pp.24/25 & 27 © Alan Gordon/Highland Light; p.30 courtesy of Glenfinnan Station Museum, © Dr. John Cooper Smith; p.59 (both) © Laurie Campbell; pp.72/73 © Ian Evans/Mountain Images; p.79 © Les Davidson

Text © Colin Nutt

ISBN 978-1-906549-04-6

Front cover: Glenfinnan; p.1: rhododendrons; p.4: detail of Bonnie Prince Charlie statue, Glenfinnan; this page: detail of remaining part of the fort, Fort William; back cover: Ben Nevis from Corpach.

For a list of websites and phone numbers please turn over >

Websites and phone numbers (where available) in the order they appear in this book:

Lochaber: www.lochaber.com
Fort William: www.visit-fortwilliam.co.uk
West Highland Museum: www.westhighlandmuseum.org.uk (T) 01397 702169
Inverlochy Castle: www.historic-scotland.gov.uk
Glen Nevis Visitor Centre: www.highland.gov.uk (T) 01397 705922
Treasures of the Earth: www.discover-fortwilliam.com (T) 01397 772283
Caledonian Canal: www.scottishcanals.co.uk (T) 0141 332 6936
Fingal Cruises: www.fingal-cruising.co.uk (T) 01397 772167
Nevis Range Mountain Resort: www.nevisrange.co.uk (T) 01397 705825
Creag Meagaidh Nature Reserve: www.snh.org.uk (T) 01528 544265
Commando Museum: commando.speanbridgehotel.co.uk (T) 0800 619 9462
Knoydart: www.knoydart-foundation.com (T) 01687 462242
Road to the Isles: www.road-to-the-isles.org.uk
Glenfinnan: www.nts.org.uk (T) 0844 493 2221
Glenfinnan Station Museum: www.glenfinnanstationmuseum.co.uk (T) 01397 722295
Jacobite Steam Train: www.steamtrain.info (T) 01524 737751
Mallaig Heritage Centre: www.mallaigheritage.org.uk (T) 01687 462085
Ardnamurchan: www.ardnamurchan.com
Ardnamurchan Natural History Centre: www.anhc.co.uk (T) 01972 500209
Ardnamurchan Point Lighthouse: www.ardnamurchan.u-net.com (T) 01972 510210